The Great Little DARTMOOR Book

Chips Barber
Sally Barber

Illustrations by
Jane Reynolds

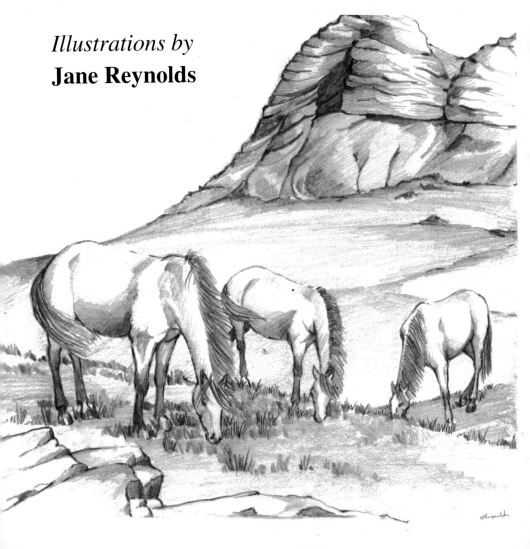

First published in 1986 (0 946651 10 8)
Reprinted in 1987, 1988, 1990, 1991 and 1992.
Revised edition printed in 1994 (0 946651 96 5)
by Obelisk Publications, 2 Church Hill, Pinhoe, Exeter, Devon
Designed by Chips and Sally Barber
Typeset by Sally Barber
Map of Dartmoor area inside front cover by Sally Barber
Printed in Great Britain by
Maslands Ltd., Tiverton Devon.

The Great Little Dartmoor Book

PREHISTORIC DARTMOOR

"As old as the hills" is a very appropriate expression for Dartmoor as these ancient, stone-littered hills were formed about 400 million years ago. Man, since the Early Bronze Age, has exploited the Moor in many ways, and the visitor to Dartmoor will see various signs of Man's dealings with the Moor – the end product being the Moor that we love today. This little book will tell just some of Dartmoor's tales and hopefully give the new enthusiast a taste of what this forbidding Moor is all about.

We should start at the beginning. All over the Moor are granite relics, some thousands of years old, others only decades. Sometimes it is hard to tell how old a granite cross may be as it always has a time-worn appearance. However, with these notes to guide you, the mists of time may clear away to give a clearer picture of Dartmoor and what it's all about.

Dartmoor's stone rows are numerous and usually culminate at a stone circle. The largest known stone row in the world runs for two miles from Stall Moor on Southern Dartmoor. The stone circle at its end is called 'The Dancers'. Many circles, composed of several upright stones, encircled a burial mound to suggest that the stone rows provided an avenue for a funeral procession to follow, but the larger circles exhibit no connection with the burial of the dead.

A kistvaen is a burial chamber made of flat stones and originally it would have been covered with earth. Many of the kistvaens on the Moor would appear, at first glance, to be too small to house a skeleton but it should be remembered that the dead were often buried in a bent-over posture. In some cases, when cremation had first taken place, the ashes of the deceased would have been buried in an urn. Unfortunately, many kistvaens have been despoiled in recent centuries, a grave matter indeed!

A cromlech usually consists of a great flat stone supported by three or more upright stones, like the fine example shown, which is Spinsters' Rock, near Drewsteignton. Sometimes a cromlech is called a Dolmen, a word taken from the French language (they are common in Brittany) – Dol means a 'table' whilst men (maen) means stone. Call them what you will, they too are megalithic remains of a burial purpose. Dartmoor has many hut circles, enough to indicate the Moor was a favourable environment in which to live in the Bronze Age period, making it one of the most densely populated areas in North West Europe. In stark contrast, today it is one of the last great wildernesses in Britain and it is possible to walk several miles without seeing another person.

The hut circles or 'pounds' (a pound was an enclosure of huts) were frequently sited on south or south west facing slopes to benefit from facing the sun on the warm sides of the hills. The huts were formed by setting stones up on end in two circles, an inner and outer ring. The cavity walling was filled with turf to give an element of weather proofing.

Poles met at the centre to form the roof whilst a canopy of thatch, made from any suitable material to hand, completed the 'detached freehold' residence. A gap in the roof was left to allow billowing smoke to escape.

The most famous hut enclosure is Grimspound, a few miles from Widecombe, which is well worth a visit. There are many other remains including menhirs, or standing stones, which are frequently found at the beginning of the stone rows. These giant monoliths are impressive, the largest on the Moor being found at Drizzlecombe (or Thrushelcombe to give it its old name) on the South-western side of the National Park.

PAST INDUSTRIES OF THE MOOR

The surface of Dartmoor is littered with the remains of past industries – the budding industrial archaeologist will have a rewarding time exploring the artefacts left as evidence of man's efforts to exploit the Moor. Apart from quarrying and mining the Moor has yielded a surprising range of items.

The drawing depicts the engine house of Wheal Betsy, a familiar landmark on the Tavistock to Okehampton road near Mary Tavy. Wheal is an old Celtic word for a mine and was commonly used in both Devon and Cornwall. Other examples are Wheal Emma, Wheal Jewell, Wheal Friendship (but not Wheal Meet Again!) Seriously though, this mine situated on the edge of the Moor was an important one that produced lead and silver. Although parking is difficult, a visit is recommended to see the spoil waste heaps as well as the plaque on it, which gives further details of its former importance. On the road side is a long line of stones known locally

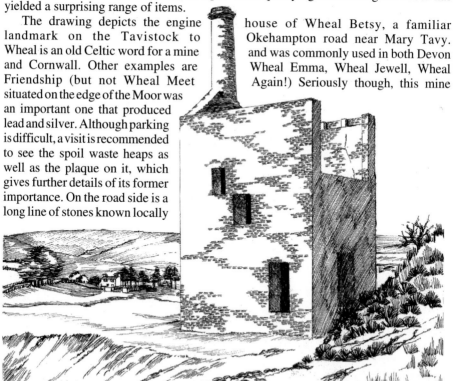

as Annie Pinkham's men. You can find out more about them in *Weird and Wonderful Dartmoor*.

One of the most important past industries was tin mining, an industry that employed rough and tough men. Almost everywhere on the Moor you will find the remains of tinners' endeavours. The early tin miners were nick named, by the later tin miners, the 'old men'. They worked the streams whilst later miners burrowed in the bowels of the earth for 'lodes' (layers) of tin.

Tin ore was processed at Blowing Houses, smallish buildings set near fast flowing streams. A head of water was diverted into a watercourse called a leat, which ran to the top of a waterwheel. As the wheel turned it provided power for a crushing mechanism to reduce the ore to a finer material. The wheel also powered a bellows to heat the ores so that the metal, now in a molten form, could flow out into mould stones where it cooled to the form of solid ingots, usually several  hundred pounds in weight. At an appointed time the tin was taken to a Stannary Town to be weighed, checked (assayed) and sold. Ashburton, Tavistock, Chagford and Plympton all served this function. Much of the tin was used in the making of pewter, one use for which was tankards.

Almost half way between Postbridge and Two Bridges, along the B3212, you will notice a row of terraced cottages. If you stop and look more closely you may be able to see the remains of some heavy duty buildings and a large chimney stack. This is the Powdermills, formerly a gunpowder factory where, between 1844 and 1872, more than 100 people were employed in the manufacture of the highly explosive substance known as Black Powder. Not all the men made gunpowder – there were carpenters, blacksmiths, coopers, carpenters and even a teacher! With a mixture of 75% potassium nitrate, 15% charcoal and 10% sulphur the end product was achieved by grinding the raw materials to a fine powder using grindstones, again turned by water power. The chimneys carried away fumes and sparks. That was the theory – in reality they occasionally didn't and explosions were quite common – the absence of roofs on the buildings is evidence of past accidents. The invention of dynamite, by the Swede, Alfred Nobel, in 1867, put paid to this unusual Dartmoor industry.

The wilder, higher and more inaccessible parts of Dartmoor boast a good cover of peat, a rich black member of the coal family. Moormen holding the right of turbary could cut and remove peat from the Moor to heat their homes or fuel blowing houses. It was even used for making a type of gas called naptha, produced on the southern Moor at Shipley Bridge and also at Princetown. Ashburton's street lights were once powered by naptha gas!

But it is not the coal black peat which people think of as the main ingredient of the Dartmoor landscape, it is the great grey granite rocks that are strewn across the Moor. Granite's uses are numerous especially as a building stone – walls, pavements, houses, churches, cottages and a host of various constructions are formed of this highly durable substance. The first granite used was simply taken from the surface of the Moor and was called moorstone by the moormen. When larger and better quality granites were desired quarrying provided an answer, the most productive sources being either in the Merrivale area, which still boasts the only working quarry today, or around Haytor on the Eastern Moor.

Granite is a difficult rock to cut through. Although today tungsten carbide or diamond-tipped saws can slice through it, the most popular method of splitting the granite was the feather and tare method. A series of drilled holes had tares or metal spikes placed in them, wedged by the feathers. Several impacts of great power were required to split the rock. At each great blow somebody had to hold the tare and feathers in place – presumably that person had a very trusting nature and nerves of steel!

Other industries that have been tried on Dartmoor include the manufacture of ice, starch, cider and glass and the production of timber and potatoes, the mining of lead, silver, copper, zinc, iron, wolfram, arsenic and granulite, and the quarrying of china clay.

In addition to this, mosses and lichens were removed from Dartmoor in the 19th century for commercial uses. Most of this was used for dye making. Sedge was also gathered and used in the making of mattresses. Now that the Moor is far less productive, preservationists will probably sleep more peacefully.

DARTMOOR—ITS TORS AND GRANITE COUNTRY

There are more than 200 tors of various shapes and sizes on Dartmoor. You can find out more about these amazing masses in *The A to Z of Dartmoor Tors*. The larger masses closest to the main roads are visited by thousands of visitors every year. These great ancient rocks would appear to have some form of magnetic fascination as families flock to climb and scramble over tors like Haytor, Hound Tor and Sharp Tor. These three all have well-worn paths leading to them.

Hound Tor has often been used for location filming, *The Hound of the Baskervilles* and *Jamaica Inn* being just two examples. Although Conan Doyle's famous story was set on Dartmoor, Daphne Du Maurier's 'Jamaica Inn' is actually on Bodmin Moor in Cornwall! Further details can be found in *Made in Devon*.

About half a mile from Hound Tor is the queer rock idol of Bowerman's Nose, a thirty-foot high figure of stone believed to be the petrified remains of Bowerman the Hunter. Legend has it that he upset the witches of Dartmoor by driving his pack through one of their secret moorland gatherings. Incensed by the intrusion, they contrived a plan to trap him. One of the witches became a hare and led Bowerman a

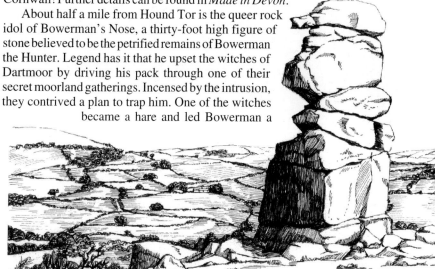

merry chase across the expanses of the Moor. She then lured him into a trap where all the witches heaped their spells on him in a fearful frenzy. The tower of rock you see is Bowerman petrified for immortality whilst the boulders around are his hounds. Geologists render a more sober, less imaginative hypothesis over its origins.

The term 'logan stone' refers to slabs of granite, or lumps of stone, which are so p r e c a r i o u s l y balanced that they will rock or pivot on their point of b a l a n c e.

Therefore a small amount of pressure can often make a boulder of many tons rock most alarmingly. Many of Dartmoor's logans in the past were traditionally used by the local population for crushing their nuts (the edible type) at Christmas. However many of the recognized logans on Dartmoor have lost their point of balance and no longer rock. Several, like the one on Rippon Tor, have been spoilt.

Haytor Rock is located on the eastern side of Dartmoor, with commanding views across South Devon. It is possible to spy Teignmouth and the Teign Estuary, Torquay, Berry Head at Brixham and much of the South Hams from this

vantage point. To the east the upper suburbs of Exeter can be identified. Beyond Exeter the cliffs near Lyme Regis can be seen on a clear day.

Thousands of people visit these rocks every year and the paths up to them are so worn that they can be seen from many miles away. It is a fact that Man, by his relentless climbing

and scrambling over the rock, is wearing the extremely hard granite away faster than the natural eroding agents of wind, ice, frost or rain.

Beneath and beyond the rocks of Haytor are many disused granite quarries. From them leads a unique tramway with many of the original rails still intact. The lines were made of granite and even the points system was formed of stone. An eight mile long trackway, opened in September 1820, stretched from this lofty elevation, almost 1,500 feet above sea level, down and around the hills to the Bovey Basin more than 1,300 feet below. The granites quarried from here went to construct such famous edifices as the British Museum, London Bridge and Nelson's Column. Production ceased in the face of stiff competition from more easily accessible Cornish granites.

Jolly Lane Cott, at Hexworthy, is a more humble granite building with an interesting history behind it. The drawing depicts it as it was soon after it was built in a single day, Midsummer's Day 1835, by Tom and Sally Satterley, with a little help from their friends. The couple had secreted away, in hedges and ditches, all the materials necessary to build the dwelling. When the local gentry went off to the Holne Ram Roasting ceremony they got to work and built the single storey cottage before sunset. To fulfil the legal requirement of claiming a freehold, they had to have smoke coming out of the chimney as well, which they did – even though it was the height of summer. The original building

survives, but with another storey added. It is the only surviving House in a Day residence on Dartmoor, and possibly in England.

BEAUTY SPOTS

The very high amount of rainfall means that many streams and rivers flow from Dartmoor in almost every conceivable direction. When Dartmoor was originally formed it was a raised plateau but, through the ages, the various watercourses have cut deep into the landscape to leave the original plateau heavily indented – a landscape of rolling hills and deep valleys. And now the deep vales, with their fast flowing streams, have become

places where people like to spend a pleasant few hours. Most visitors, looking for a relaxing time, will be content to explore those riverside venues that are sufficiently close to a road or car park. Thus it tends to be this combination of riverside and vehicle access that unites to make 'beauty spots'. Visitors to the Moor on fine summer days will notice the gregarious streak in people at places like Dartmeet, Huccaby, Postbridge, Cadover, Becky Falls (pictured here) and Fingle Bridge. Anyone reading this little book at one of these beauty spots need only to walk a few hundred yards along the river bank to find more secluded surroundings in which to sit in relative peace.

Becky Falls is a waterfall attraction where the wooded Becka Brook plunges over a ravine of enormous boulders. In a wet season it is a particularly spectacular sight but after a dry spell there is more rock than water. It is a popular venue, being handily located on the favoured eastern side of Dartmoor within a few miles of both Haytor and Widecombe. Downstream there are several more waterfalls, but access to them involves some strenuous exercise over giant boulders. Becky Falls is fairly well sheltered on windy days and energetic visitors can enjoy a scramble over the many rocks. There is both a gift shop and a cafe.

Postbridge must be the best known landmark on Dartmoor. The clapper bridge

comprises four piers with four great slabs. The top is seven feet above the East Dart River and is over 40 feet long. It is an excellent example of its type and originally lay on a major track that crossed the Moor long before the age of motorized vehicles. Postbridge has a few places where refreshment can be obtained and a Dartmoor Tourist Information centre where you can find out all the things omitted from this guide. For those people who like to walk there is a lovely, small waterfall about one and a half miles north west of Postbridge on the East Dart River. A map and compass should be taken, just in case a sudden mist descends without warning. The ground beside the East Dart is often marshy and stout shoes should be worn. Failing that a pair of water wings might be useful!

Cadover Bridge is on the south western side of Dartmoor and is favoured by Plymothians, as it is only a short drive away from their city. On a fine day it bears all the appearances of a seaside resort, with the River Plym replacing the sea. The spot itself is not particularly beautiful but the Moor nearby is easily accessible and

the wooded gorge of the Plym, below it, is well worth a visit. The wooded walk down to Shaugh Bridge, another well patronized spot, is a lovely ramble. (It is also walk No 4 in *Ten Family Walks on Dartmoor*.)

Dartmeet is the point where the East and West Dart Rivers unite. Many years ago Dartmeet was the summer camp for a large group of gypsies who spent their winters in the Dartmoor border towns. Badgers Holt

has a long established reputation for fine teas and is an excellent place to stop for refreshments on this part of Dartmoor.

Fingle Bridge is one of the most beautiful of all the Dartmoor beauty spots. Unlike the previously mentioned places it is not on the open Moor but lies just within the National Park boundary on the borderland. The River Teign enters a six mile long gorge a few miles from Chagford. Fingle Bridge, spanning the Teign, is in this deep wooded valley. The valley is excellent for short walks, the most popular strolls being the Fishermen's Path, along the river banks – an easy and enjoyable track, and the more strenuous journey along the Hunters' Path. This climbs from Fingle Bridge and gives views towards Castle Drogo and the distant high Moors of Northern Dartmoor. A combination of the two makes an excellent circular outing. One cautionary word, if you have a picnic at Fingle Bridge beware of red ants – the whole of the gorge is populated by them.

The Anglers Rest at Fingle Bridge is well worth a visit. Look out for the wooden fish on the walls, replicas of specimens taken from the Teign.

Lydford Gorge is in the good hands of the National Trust so an admission charge is made to this spectacular feature. The River Lyd cascades into the deep ravine of the gorge, an awesome sight after days of heavy and prolonged rainfall. At such times a walk through it is not an experience for the faint-hearted because the path is steep and narrow. The rewards for such endeavour include the 100 feet high White Lady waterfall. Another feature, 'The Devil's Cauldron', conjures up an image of frenzied water and is an impressive sight after heavy rain.

Three centuries ago a den of thieves inhabited this gorge. They were called the Gubbins and were by led by Roger Rowle, an evil scallywag who was immortalized in Charles Kingsley's *Westward Ho!* Rowle has been dubbed the Robin Hood of the West whilst his band of red-haired cattle thieves have been labelled the Doones of Dartmoor. Their thieving missions could not have brought too many riches for they are reputed to have lived in holes dug in the ground.

PRINCETOWN

It could be argued that when people from 'up country' think of 'Dartmoor', it is the prison at Princetown that they picture. Every year thousands of visitors come to gaze at the drab grey complex of buildings known as HM Prison Dartmoor. Princetown itself is an isolated town set in a bleak and inhospitable landscape.

Originally the prison was built for French Prisoners of War. Hundreds of Frenchmen had been captured in the Napoleonic Wars and were held in six large boats, moored at Plymouth, in conditions so terrible that mutiny threatened. With Devonport and its arsenal close by, alternative accommodation was sought, and a spot on the Moors about 16 miles distant seemed the perfect solution.

At the instigation of Thomas Tyrwhitt, an MP for Plymouth, the prison was constructed on the Moor, some 1,430 feet above sea level and sufficiently distant from civilization to deter would-be absconders. However, when completed and populated by 7,000 prisoners and 500 troops, conditions were grimmer than ever. The extremes of Dartmoor weather inflicted severe hardships on the inmates; life 'inside' was tough and uncompromising. Amongst the prisoners was a group of men called 'Les Romans', the dregs of French society. They were the roughest, toughest and most bestial beings ever seen at Princetown. They foraged through refuse for scraps and, on one occasion, when a horse led a cart to collect rubbish they set on it, hacked it to pieces and devoured the raw, still palpitating, flesh. American

Prisoners of War arrived and records reveal that 212 soldiers and sailors died there in 1812. A memorial gateway at the entrance to the American POW cemetery was erected in 1928 by the 'National Society of the United States Daughters of 1812'.

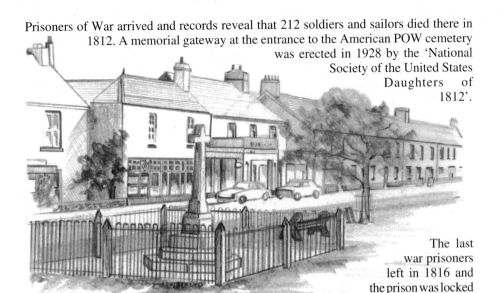

The last war prisoners left in 1816 and the prison was locked up and left disused for almost half a century. In the dormant years several suggestions for its future were suggested, such as a school of industry for orphans and juvenile offenders. For a short time it was a factory using Dartmoor peat to make naptha gas. However, with Australian penal colonies refusing to accept any more English convicts a need arose for a large prison on British soil, and so HM Prison Dartmoor was established.

In its Victorian heyday it was regarded as the toughest British prison and earned the description of 'Halfway to Hell'. Prisoners erring from the straight and narrow were often restrained by ball and chain, leg irons handcuffs or even strait jackets. Birchings were common as were floggings with a cat o' nine tails for serious misdeeds. This 'jovial' scene was enhanced by the diet of bread and water!

During the Great War many prisoners 'escaped' after electing to fight for their country and nearly 300 were killed in the process. The road across the Moor to Two Bridges is often referred to as 'Conchies Road' as it was built by the 'Conchies', conscientious

objectors, who took the place of the convicts but were treated much better.

Escape bids from the prison have been made on many occasions, sometimes with real enterprise. In 1928 a man stole a Roman Catholic priest's vestments and his car; people waved to him as he drove off – mistaking him for Father Finnegin. However, he remained at large for just two days. Several years later a Church of England vicar's clerical garb and car were stolen. This time the criminal neglected to change his distinctive prison boots, which protruded so prominently from beneath his tunic that he too was quickly arrested.

The main deterrent in preventing escape bids is the problem of getting off the Moor. When the mist is down it is almost impossible to make a straight course, without the aid of a compass, and hours may be spent covering the same territory. One escapee spent five days on the Moor before unwittingly stumbling back into Princetown. Further unusual escapes are featured in *Weird and Wonderful Dartmoor*.

The town of Princetown lives on the reputation and 'fame' of the prison. It draws the visitors and they can buy (from the gift shops and not the prison!) a vast range of 'prison' souvenirs – suitably decorated mugs, teatowels, etc.

The town is generally unattractive in its architecture and is an unenviable place in which to live. Fortunately it has several redeeming features in the shape of its various pubs, and the excellent High Dartmoor Interpretation Centre situated in the former Duchy Hotel where it is believed that Conan Doyle penned the basis of his famous novel, *The Hound of the Baskervilles*.

WATER SUPPLIES

Rainfall has to be a curse for Princetown's residents – it has almost four times the annual rainfall of London – but to the great number of Plymothians, it is a veritable blessing. The rain, which gives birth to so many streams and rivers, is the lifeblood of a city that has drawn its supply from the Moor since 1590.

The legendary Sir Francis Drake engineered a leat from the Moor down to Plymouth to ensure a clean and reliable supply of water. The River Meavy gave a south-west flow of water for Drake to build 'Drake's Leat'. It served the town well for a few centuries but a more reliable source was sought. As a result the Devonport Leat was constructed, taking its water from the Blackbrook, West Dart and Cowsic (an awful name for a river). This seventeen mile long watercourse wends its way around the hills passing close to the notorious Foxtor Mires on its way towards Plymouth. Arthur Conan Doyle based his Grimpen Mire on Foxtor Mires, an area of exquisite dampness guaranteed to trap even the most fleet-footed of boghoppers.

By contrast the relatively firm ground beside the Devonport Leat affords a safe corridor across the Moor. Those who follow the public sections of the leat for a walk will not go far wrong, provided that they don't have the misfortune to fall in! Humans should not have much to fear, other than a 'British Standard Bootful' of icy water. Animals in a similar situation find it a much more traumatic experience and usually need a helping hand to get out.

The leat passes an old water-filled mine working known as Crazywell or Classiwell Pool. Legend says it is bottomless and even the combined lengths of the bell ropes of nearby Walkhampton Church, when knotted together, would not reach the bottom. Paddling is not recommended!

The leat plunges down Raddick Hill, crosses the Meavy and heads towards Dousland, a village that still derives much of its water from this watercourse. Below this stretch lies Burrator Reservoir, still Plymouth's main source of water. The reservoir was the first to be built on Dartmoor and was opened in 1898. Even then there were preservationists fighting to

prevent part of a moorland valley from being drowned. This has continued to be the case throughout the twentieth century with reservoirs on Dartmoor now supplying the needs of a high proportion of Devon's population. Meldon Reservoir, near Okehampton, supplies North Devon whilst Venford Reservoir supplies Paignton. Totnesians and natives of the South Hams get their water from the Avon Dam, a few miles above South Brent. Torquinians (residents of Torquay) rely on Fernworthy Reservoir near Chagford and the beautiful triple reservoir of Tottiford, Trenchford and Kennick a few miles from Bovey Tracey.

Several of these reservoirs are surrounded by large coniferous plantations and there are some excellent waymarked trails at Kennick and Fernworthy. The Forest trails at Bellever, a mile from Postbridge, also make a pleasant safari, particularly when high winds prevail on the open Moor.

The tomb of Childe the Hunter lies on the edge of the notorious mire known as Foxtor

Mires, three miles south of Princetown. A planned reservoir for this site was defeated by the Dartmoor Preservation Association.

In the times of Edward III Childe, a hunter from Plymstock was out on the Moor, lost in a raging blizzard. He killed his horse, disembowelled it, and crept inside the shelter of its carcass. Aware of his predicament, he is supposed to have left a message, in his horse's blood, stating that whoever took him to his grave should inherit all his extensive lands at Plymstock. This prompted a race between the Abbeys of Tavistock and Plymstock to see who could secure his body and thus his estate. An action-packed drama involving ambushes and all

manner of underhand tricks ensued until the monks of Tavistock triumphed. Childe must have been a fool to have killed the one creature who would have kept him alive with its warmth, and, left to its own devices, would probably have taken him home!

BOVEY TRACEY

The ever-busy small town of Bovey Tracey lies just outside the boundary of the Dartmoor National Park, and from many points in and around it the high hills of the Moor tower above it. Most locals simply refer to the town as Bovey (pronounced "Buvvy"), the same name as the river that flows from the Moors, past the town, to join the River Teign a few miles downstream. The Traceys were the Lords of the Manor and it is believed that one member of this family had a hand in the murder of Thomas Becket.

The arrival of the railway in 1866 developed the town's reputation as a good centre from which to explore the Moors. The Great Western Railway once ran their own bus service from Bovey Tracey Station to Haytor or Becky Falls and, also in the season, ran excursions to many of the familiar moorland haunts. Sadly the railway was closed in 1959 but the fortuitous siting of the town, ideally positioned for the Moors, and the South Devon coast, just a few miles from the A38, has helped maintain its role as a centre for visitors.

The town is steeped in history and is certainly worth a visit. Driving from one end of the town to the other end is not always easy but there are plenty of places to seek refreshment and recover from the 'joys' of motoring. The geology of the immediate hills shaped not only the landscape but also the main occupations. The extensive clay beds of the adjacent Bovey Basin (an ancient lake) have enabled many associated industries to develop, such as a brickworks and several potteries.

Around Bovey there are many public footpaths. Those that rise into the hills will reward the explorer with many stunning views and some interesting safaris. The area in the vicinity of Tottiford, Trenchford and Kennick, in particular, is countryside at its best. It has often been referred to as "Little Switzerland in Devon". Yodelling is optional.

LUSTLEIGH

The village of Lustleigh is located in a deep bowl in the hills on the south eastern margin of the Moor. The country roundabout is not as wild and open as the higher moorlands but is bestowed with fine woodlands and some enormous granite boulders, which appear in the most unlikely of locations. This countryside has a veritable maze of public paths, all well signposted, that weave around the village to form a complicated but highly enjoyable network for the casual walker to explore.

Lustleigh has many interesting buildings. The old vestry is the site where William Davy and his servant put together and printed, on their own printing press, 26 volumes called "A System of Divinity".

Another interesting building is the splendid Cleave Hotel, a former farmhouse. What was presumably one of its fields during its days as a farm, is now the village cricket field. To find such a flat track in such a hilly area is most unusual and it certainly makes a very attractive sporting arena.

The well known, and equally well photographed, cross on the village green was erected in memory of Henry Tudor (no relation to past Kings of England) who was rector for a spell of 16 years at the turn of the century.

The River Wrey runs through Lustleigh. It follows a fault valley downwards from the vicinity of Moretonhampstead. The natural corridor carved out of the landscape was ideal for railway engineers who constructed a branch line from Newton Abbot through Lustleigh up to Moreton. The line closed in 1959 after 93 years of service. When the first version of *The Hounds of the Baskervilles* was filmed on Dartmoor several scenes were shot there. However it is a cat that provides an interesting little tale. It seems that the stationmaster once had a cat called Jumbo of whom he was most fond. When this poor feline friend had used up the last of his allocated lives, he was buried in a grave on the platform with an epitaph: "Beneath this slab and laid out flat lies Jumbo, once our station cat". This memorial no longer exists and the station has been converted into a private dwelling.

A good location for a picnic is the village orchard. Here there is an enormous stone with the names of many young ladies carved upon the rock. A little seat is where the May Queen is crowned each year. The ceremony originally took place at the nearby ancient Wreyland Manor. In recent years the events have occurred on the first Saturday in May. The colourful pageant assembles and wends it way through the village, pauses for a short service on the church steps, and leads on to the crowning ceremony in the Town Orchard. To add colour to the spectacle, Morris dancing and tripping around the Maypole complete the proceedings.

Lustleigh, and the surrounding environs, will provide the more discerning visitor with a pleasant time. You will not find the trappings of tourism overtly displayed here.

BUCKLAND IN THE MOOR

This hamlet has long been a favourite for photographers, with its cluster of cottages set in sylvan surroundings, composing an idyllic picture. It is probably seen at its best in the days of late Autumn when sunlight illuminates the scene and the leaves turn to gold. The countryside around Buckland is some of Dartmoor's finest but much of the woodland is private so it is advisable to follow either signposted public rights of way, or stick to the open commons high above this hamlet.

The small church of St Peter at Buckland in the Moor is celebrated in guide books and gazetteers for its unusual clockface, which has the words 'My Dear Mother' spelt out instead of normal numerals.

The rocky pinnacle high above Buckland is called Buckland Beacon, easily reached

on foot from Cold East Cross. The land falls away spectacularly to the south-west, with expansive views from this fine vantage point. On the rocky summit of Buckland Beacon are two slabs that have the Ten Commandments engraved on them. Unfortunately the wind, rain and other weathering factors have made the words far harder to decipher than when they were etched into the rocks in the summer of 1928. At the behest of Mr Whitley, of Welstor, Arthur Clement, from Exmouth, spent several weeks carving the words onto the slabs. The work was carried out to celebrate the defeat, in Parliament, of the Revised Prayer Book.

WIDECOMBE

Widecombe is a famous village by virtue of an old folk song well known for its characters – Tom Pearse (or Pearce), Bill Brewer, Jan Stewer, Peter Gurney, Peter Davy, Dan'l Whidden, Harry Hawk, old Uncle Tom Cobley (or Cobleigh) and all. These folk still live on, captured for all time on postcards, and a host of knickknacks designed to perpetuate the legend. The song was first published in 1880 by Mr W. Davies of Kingsbridge but was popularized nine years later by Sabine Baring Gould in his 'Songs and Ballads of the West'. Since then the song and the village have enjoyed much publicity. The song has been sung by many artists and in many languages – including Japanese (the mind boggles). The Devonshire Regiment gave a hearty rendition of the song just before going into battle during the South Africa War at the turn of this century.

And thus, within the shadow of a legend, this little moorland village greets hundreds of thousands of visitors each year. The village is nestled deep in the East Webburn valley but the church spire of St Pancras rises heavenwards and provides a distinctive feature in the landscape. Visitors to the church will notice the story of a disaster that befell the church on 21 October 1638 when a terrible thunderstorm broke over the village. The church was badly damaged and a fireball, which burst through it, killed four people, and severely injured another thirty of the congregation; people in some seats were scorched whilst others just feet away escaped unhurt. The Devil was blamed for this carnage in revenge for a broken pact made with a local man, Jan Reynolds of Birch Tor.

Virtually every guide book to Dartmoor uses the phrase 'Cathedral of the Moor' to describe Widecombe's spectacular church of St Pancras. With its lofty, distinctive 120-foot high tower, it looks so majestic, and is a very prominent feature in the landscape. Its grandeur, quite out of keeping with the size of its community, can be attributed to the prosperity of the tin mining industry, which dominated the Dartmoor landscape in past centuries. The tower has been compared with that of Magdalen College at Oxford and is one of the finest in South West England. Evidence of the tin mining association can be seen in the curious carving of the three rabbits, the tinners' symbol,

which is in the roof. Look closely and you will see that the rabbits suffer from a shortage of ears.

Near the church stands an old yew tree where, in the past, foxes shot or killed within the parish, were displayed. It seems that the 'bounty hunters' made a real killing as they received four times more for a dead fox in Widecombe than at neighbouring Ashburton, only six miles away. Other creatures, which also had a bounty on them, included badgers, polecats and even hedgehogs.

The Church House, owned by the National Trust, was originally built about 1500, and has seen many changes of use. People travelling to Widecombe's Church often had a wearying journey of many miles and the church house offered rest facilities. Throughout the country many of these church houses were later 'converted' to pubs, which accounts for the great number of inns bearing the name the Church House Inn. This one, however, between 1878-1932 was the village school and now, under the auspices of the National Trust, it sells high quality merchandise to the many visitors who browse around Widecombe. Perhaps one reason why the Church House never became an inn was because there was already one opposite. The Old Inn, with its colourful but obvious inn sign above the main door, goes back to the fourteenth century but a dreadful fire in January 1977 almost prevented it from seeing out the twentieth century. An electrical fault, and not the Devil, was held to blame on this occasion.

Widecombe's permanent population is about 600 but the majority are scattered around the immense parish of 11,000 acres. Many live in farms and hamlets in the shelter of the East Webburn's wide valley – hence the name 'wide combe' (combe means valley). The village has never topped 1,000 residents but came closest to doing so in 1851 where 974 people lived there.

The most photographed feature in Widecombe is the stone village sign naming 'Widecombe in the Moor', which stands on the grass verge by the church. If you stand and watch other visitors you will observe that it is regularly snapped as proof of a visit to this famous spot. Originally it stood on the village green but was taken down in 1939 in case of invasion (from the Germans and not tourists). Then it was made of tiles but it was broken beyond repair whilst being moved. The present landmark goes back to 1948 when local man Francis Hamlyn donated this carving of Uncle Tom and friends. It is set in Horton greenstone, was designed by the great Dartmoor preservationist Lady Sylvia Sayer and was built by Knight of Newton Abbot. The granite base was built by the Widecombe mason Mr Thomas Nosworthy.

The village green at Widecombe is that area cordoned off by granite boulders, the grassy area that has to be crossed between the car park and the gift shops. Centuries ago it was an area where the villagers practised their archery. An Act of Parliament in 1466 obliged every inhabitant to shoot on feast days. If they failed to do so they were fined. Earlier this century travelling shows and other entertainments appeared on the green but today the festivities seem to be restricted to Widecombe Fair Day. Widecombe Fair takes place on the second Tuesday in September. Despite the peak tourist season being well over, crowds flock to the village and the moorland roads resemble London in the rush hour.

We started our brief look at Widecombe by mentioning the story of how Tom Pearse lent a number of associates his poor old grey mare so they could make their way to Widecombe to enjoy great celebrations and alcoholic revelry. Most of the motley crew came from the village of Spreyton, almost 20 miles north of Widecombe. This village, a 'one horse town' (but not the grey mare!) has not evolved into a tourist centre like the famous Widecombe. However there are plenty of reminders that the song, and its story, has its roots there. The pub is called 'The Tom Cobley' and there are several variations of the theme found in the names of the cottages and houses. In the churchyard is a stone of a Thomas Cobley who may, or may not, be the legendary character in the ill-fated tale.

The countryside around Widecombe is full of variety with some fine tors dominating the hillsides. If you stand in Widecombe and look up to the skyline you will see tors like Chinkwell, Honeybag, Bell, Top, Hollow and Pil Tor all on the same ridge. A walk along this ridge is a pleasant and easy jaunt. The view back down to Widecombe is almost as spectacular as looking down from an aeroplane. There are many attractive hamlets in this corner of eastern Dartmoor, perhaps none more beautiful than Ponsworthy.

Ponsworthy is a hamlet on the West Webburn River a few miles from Widecombe. The beauty of the granite cottages set beyond the ford has prompted photographers and artists alike to capture it down the years, a scene of rustic charm and subtle beauty.

BUCKFAST ABBEY

It is said that Buckfast had an abbey before England had a king. However, it should be clearly stated that the present abbey is a modern edifice and was only completed in 1938. It is built within the grounds of a former abbey, which dated back to 1018, but was a victim of the dissolution in the reign of Henry VIII.

Buckfast Abbey is a most impressive building and the story of its construction is a tale of toil and struggle. Not resorting to the modern tactic of a public appeal for funds, Abbot Vonier had only meagre resources at his disposal, a sovereign and an old horse and cart. In addition he had a monk who knew how to build and was able to teach fellow monks his skills. So in 1906 a small band of monks set to work to build it themselves! Fortunately stone was plentiful in the vicinity and a lady of substance provided much of the necessary raw materials. Another person supplied a horse and a friendly neighbour provided all the necessary building sand. Although never more than six men had been working on the Abbey it was two thirds complete by 1922. Abbot Vonier died a few weeks after its completion in 1938. A tour of the Abbey is an enjoyable and refreshing experience. The legendary Buckfast honey and tonic wine provide the perfect excuse for a visit, should you need an excuse.

CHAGFORD

The ancient borderland town of Chagford is a place of enormous activity and life – a town far busier than its population of 1,500 would suggest. Located on the moorland fringe, it draws people from a wide area because of its charm and its excellent shops. Indicative of the town's prosperity is the large number of places where liquid and solid refreshment can be acquired. Amongst the hostelries is The Bullers Arms (formerly the Bakers Arms), The Ring O'Bells and The Three Crowns.

The signs proclaim Chagford as an ancient stannary town, which dates back to at least 1305. Its name, when translated, means Gorse Ford, presumably where the River Teign could be crossed near gorse-covered moorland. No doubt the enormous Meldon Hill, which towers above the town, extended its rough vegetation down to the Teign.

In recent decades the town has attracted many wealthy retired folk, people wise enough to see that this country town is the perfect place for a quiet life away from the madding crowds and distractions of city life. Not that Chagford is so much of a backwater. Yeo Farm is believed to have been the first in Britain to have electric power by courtesy of a waterwheel. John Perryman developed a supply that worked not only lights but, with the aid of belts and pulleys, all | sorts of farm equipment.

It is hard to imagine that | Chagford was a mining town but there are
well-hidden remains of mines | around the district. In the 16th century tinners
toiled at mines like Bulshill, | Broomhill and Westcott. Better methods of
extraction were available to the | miners who worked at Great Week at the
turn of this century. Quality | cassiterite or tin ore was extracted and sold
in London at a good price. | However as Chagford had become
important in other ways it was | not such a death knell to the town's
economy when the mine | closed in 1902.

Another industry that | enabled Chagford to thrive was that of
wool. With a vast | population of sheep grazing on the

nearby moorlands it was a natural location for a woollen factory. This was located beside the Teign, and between 1800-1848 it manufactured blankets. Despite the workers 'spinning a good yarn', lack of demand closed this industry. The people of Chagford were obviously adaptable and, although the population declined after this, they pulled themselves together and built up a healthy trade as an inland resort where hunting, fishing and shooting created plenty of employment. There were elaborate plans to bring the railroad to Chagford by way of the lovely Teign Gorge, and had this route been executed it would have been one of wanton recklessness. Fortunately visitors availed themselves of the branch line terminus at nearby Moretonhampstead to complete the journey by horse drawn carriage or, in later times, motorbus. A bus route, believed to be the earliest rural service in Devon, operated from Exeter to Chagford – an indication of Chagford's importance and a desire by a rival railway company to win a share of moorland-bound passengers.

The number of inns, places for refreshment and hotels reflects Chagford's continuing prowess as a centre for exploring Dartmoor, by car, by pony or on foot. A walk across Padley Common and up the gigantic Meldon Hill gives the best view of the Chagford countryside. Do not underestimate the 'climb' and if you do attempt it, spare a thought for all the golfers who once played the nine holes that contoured the side of the hill. The

The Great Little Dartmoor Book

course closed earlier this century possibly because the local golfing fraternity found that the added dimension of mountaineering was too much of a handicap. Nevertheless the hill is capped by some extremely fine and rugged rockpiles, pleasant eyries in which to sit and inspect the far horizons of distant Exmoor boldly outlined beyond the mid-Devon plain. If it is raining you'll be lucky if you can see Chagford at the bottom of the hill!

DREWSTEIGNTON AND CASTLE DROGO

Castle Drogo, a National Trust property near Drewsteignton, is the newest castle in England and doubtless it was known, when it was built early this century, that it would

never be called upon to be defended. The legions and armies that descend on it today are visitors and tourists who come to admire its perfect site and its clever architecture, designed for Julius Drew by the genius Sir Edwin Lutyens.

Julius Drew was born in 1856. The son of a poor clergyman, he went to China at the age of 17 and astutely realized that if he could take 'all the tea in China', or as much as was possible, direct to the British public, he would cut out the middleman, the trader, and make a 'pot' of money. He did just this and, with his fortune, joined John Musker to form the Home and Colonial Stores. And so it was at the age of 33 he retired. He employed a genealogist to trace his family's roots back to a Medieval Lord Drogo or Dru who had given his name to Drewsteignton. His uncle Richard was then Rector of Drewsteignton and Julius decided to build a castle nearby.

In 1910 Julius acquired the glebelands (lands belonging to the church), which amounted to about 450 acres of land, and employed Lutyens to build him an imaginative and romantic castle. With £50,000 to spend on the house, and another £10,000 to landscape the gardens, Lutyens started the work that was to take 20 years. The finished effort, although magnificent, was much smaller than was initially conceived. Nevertheless, by using various levels and by means of ramps, steps and vaulting a grand building was created. The grounds included a small stable block, a cottage, garage and an impressive drive.

Castle Drogo is built of local granite, a highly durable and appropriate material. The power of the River Teign, flowing hundreds of feet below, was harnessed to provide electricity for the castle. On a fine day a visit to the castle should be complemented by a walk along the Teign Gorge. The Hunters' Path, an elevated track that eventually drops down to Fingle Bridge, or the Fisherman's Path, along the banks of the Teign, are well worth pedestrian exploration. The conditions underfoot are generally firm but a little stamina may be useful for the steeper gradients. (Walk No 3 in *Ten Family Walks on Dartmoor* contains full details.)

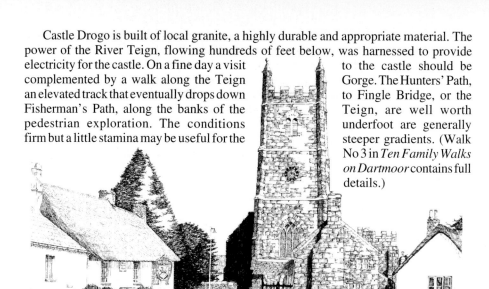

Drewsteignton is a small village with less than 600 inhabitants, less than half the population it had during the mid nineteenth century. However, its residents often live to a great old age, like the celebrated 'Aunt Mabel' or Mrs Mudge at The Drewe Arms who must have broken all records for 'longest serving landlady'. This thatched pub is unusual, like an inn from the past; it has no bar but is a place of character and characters.

STRANGE TALES OF DARTMOOR

Bedevilled by mists and almost incessant rainfall, the high land of Dartmoor is a wilderness in many respects. It is a mysterious landscape, one haunted by all sorts of weird and amazing stories, some with an element of historical truth, others (hopefully) born out of the fantasies and fiction of fellow man.

But we will start with a sad story, which has led to another more gentle mystery. In the eighteenth century a young orphan girl who was a servant at Canna Farm, became pregnant by a young man of a much higher social status. In her shame, she hanged herself in a barn. Church law decreed suicide victims should not be buried in consecrated ground but at a cross-roads, so that the troubled spirits could not find their way back. Jay's Grave, which is only a few hundred

The Great Little Dartmoor Book

yards from Hound Tor, is at a cross-roads with a track coming up from the East Webburn Valley. The drawing of the humble grave of poor Kitty Jay is shown here, complete with the fresh flowers that appear through all seasons. Nobody knows who puts them there, and nobody is telling!

A lesser known but similar story relates to Stephen's Grave, high on the Moor not far from Peter Tavy. George Stephen fell in love with the daughter of a well-to do farmer who forbade him to see the young lady. In sorrow he ate poisonous leaves and berries and collapsed dying on the Moor near the home of his loved one. His grave bears no flowers and remains a lonely landmark.

The two tales vary little in the retelling but the next one varies considerably. The 'bare bones' of this saga is that Lady Mary Howard, daughter of Sir John Fitz of Fitzford near Tavistock, was left, at the age of nine, heiress to vast estates when her father died. Her wardship was bought by the Earl of Northumberland who, cunningly, arranged a marriage between his brother, Sir Allen Percy, and Mary when she was twelve years old. Three years later Sir Allen died, aged 34, leaving Mary to marry the second son of the Earl of Suffolk, Sir Thomas Howard. Unhappy with Sir Thomas she ran away with the Earl of Rivers. However with all the spice of a good soap opera, her second husband died and she returned to marry his brother, Sir Charles Howard. They had two daughters but then poor old Sir Charles died. Not to be left on the shelf, Lady Howard married yet again, this time to Sir Richard Grenville, grandson of the great naval man. Unlike his illustrious grandfather, this Richard was an evil, unpopular man. He too bit the dust, his passing being rejoiced by many at that time. There is no proof that she murdered all four husbands but for the sake of a gruesome legend it is speculated that she did. There is a walk at Okehampton Castle called Lady Howard's Walk and it is said that a coach of bones, made up from the skeletons of the murdered men, with a headless coach driver, travels every night to Okehampton Castle. She is doomed to visit the Castle and pluck a blade of grass each night until all the blades are gone – and she can't use a mower. Some versions of the story state that she does this chore with her head tucked underneath her arm. Many stories of this type involve the victim being sentenced to perform a never ending task – Jan Tregeagale has to empty Dozmary Pool on Bodmin Moor with a sieve, and Cranmere Benjie does the same at Cranmere Pool on Dartmoor. Judging by the dryness of the latter, he seems to be well on the way (he obviously drinks Carling Black Label).

If you travel along the B3212 between Postbridge and Two Bridges you may like to keep a wary eye out for the 'Hairy Hands'. These have plagued many motorists along this stretch of road since the early part of this century. The large pair of Hairy Hands are said to grip the driver's hands and wrench the steering wheel to force him off the road. Between 1910-1920 a series of accidents, involving pony traps and cyclists, occurred which were totally unaccountable, but all featured the Hairy Hands. As cars and then motor coaches also suffered the same fate, national newspaper reporters came to investigate. A detailed inspection was made and the camber of the road was deemed to be the true culprit so repairs were made. Even so reportings of the Hairy Hands continued, even in stationary vehicles!

The mischievous pixies of Dartmoor appear to be a less harmful menace. They live in the nooks and crannies of tors on Dartmoor and have definitely been less obvious since Dartmoor Letterboxers have started searching their habitats whilst looking for letterboxes (see later). Clad in their green and red (that is the Pixies and not the 'boxers') they lead an active life on the Moor. They like to dance, often in a circle, but do not like to be watched. Should you be caught watching them you will be invited to join in and you will find it both impossible to refuse or to stop dancing – a very tiring punishment. Amongst walkers, particularly those whose mapwork or compass work is poor, a common expression invoked is 'Pixie led'. There is the inference that it is the Pixies, and not their navigational skills, which have made them lose their way. The

remedy to avoid 'pixiefication' is simple – you have to turn your clothes inside out. For those who either wish to see Pixies, or fancy a marathon dance, good locations include Hound Tor (as shown above), around Widecombe, Sheeps Tor and in the Teign Valley. Their chief occupation is shoe making and they live off moorland fruit and titbits left out for them by kindly locals. Unlike the feeding of ponies, there are no fines for doing this!

If you want to meet some pixies at first hand, you should visit 'Pixieland', a short distance up the hill from Dartmeet on the way towards Two Bridges.

The highest rockpile, from summit to base, on Dartmoor is a strange mass of granite called Vixen Tor, close to the hamlet of Merrivale. Near the tor is an area of swamp land that can be quite easily bypassed in good weather. It is this combination of mire, moorland weather and the slightly sinister-looking Vixen Tor that gives us the legend of Vixana the Witch. She was certainly an evil old hag and bore all the grim visual specifications necessary for such a role in life. She had grime-laden teeth, her hair was tangled, grey and in need of a good conditioner, and her nose was enormously long (rather like mine in fact!) All in all, she was an unattractive proposition at the best of times.

Vixana's only enjoyment in life stemmed from her hobby of luring people to a watery death in the mire near the tor. Travellers were easy prey as the track over the Moor passed nearby. She would cast a spell and summon up a thick fog. Whilst the poor traveller sank in the mire she would cackle with pleasure. Everyone was desperate to rid the Moor of this foul fiend so a handsome young moorman, who had been bestowed with wondrous powers, for helping the pixies, was approached. He had a magic ring to make himself invisible and the ability to see through the thickest fog. This made him the ideal candidate for the job of sorting out the witch. As he approached she tried to trap him but, with his special powers, he made himself invisible and crept up to the top of the tor. Seeing his chance, he caught the wicked witch by surprise and sent her crashing from the highest tor on Dartmoor, to her death.

These are just a few of the many stories and legends of Dartmoor. On a fine summer's day they seem laughable but alone, in a thick mist, on a dark night …? More strange and unusual Dartmoor stories can be found in *Dark and Dastardly Dartmoor* and *Weird and Wonderful Dartmoor*.

PUBS

It is not surprising that in an area of 365 square miles there are bound to be a vast number of inns and public houses (yippee!) Although only a small proportion are mentioned here it should be noted that the author is still, happily, researching and that a non-mention of a pub does not necessarily mean that it hasn't much to offer the weary, thirsty wayfarer. It would also be foolish to lavish praise on specific establishments as landlords come and go and thus reputations of quality and service rise and fall accordingly. Here is a brief appraisal of a small selection of inns and pubs, a random choice.

The Ring O'Bells at North Bovey is a popular spot for people who don't mind navigating along narrow, twisty lanes. The village is a lovely one with many character cottages, a village green and, should you fall off your horse, a mounting block near the inn, a relic of the day when visitors came on one horse power modes of transport.

Some inns attract unusual customers. The Tavistock Inn, at Poundsgate, on that same fateful day when

Widecombe Church was so fiercely stricken by a thunderbolt, entertained a passing rider who looked suspiciously evil. After paying for his fayre the dark rider galloped off. The landlady then discovered that his gold coins had withered into shrivelled-up leaves Obviously this must have been the Devil for everybody knows that money doesn't grow on trees! This lovely old inn is definitely worth a visit.

Perhaps the most famous inn on Dartmoor is the Warren House, which stands in splendid isolation a few miles from Postbridge on the B3212. It is one of the highest inns in England and is certainly one of the most exposed. Originally the pub existed on the other side of the road and was a welcome refuge for the many tin miners who ground out a meagre existence from the various pits in the immediate neighbourhood. The miners supplemented their diet by breeding rabbits in warrens, hence the name of the pub. The symbol for tinners is a triangle of rabbits, which will often be seen in churches of stannary towns. The pub is famous for its fire, which is said to have remained alight for many years, through all seasons.

The Church House Inn at Holne has paid host to several well-known people. Charles Kingsley author of the much acclaimed *Westward Ho!* was born at the nearby vicarage. William Crossing, one of the greatest Dartmoor writers, was a frequent guest, and it is said that Oliver Cromwell also passed some time there.

DARTMOOR'S WILDLIFE AND ANIMALS

Many of the animals that you see on Dartmoor are not wild, despite the fact that they roam the wild expanses of the Moor in apparent freedom. The ponies, cattle and sheep all belong to someone and usually carry a mark of identification. The ponies, which everybody seems to love photographing, are often to be seen hanging around car parks but are not to be fed as this encourages them to be a nuisance and potential hazard on the roads. Also, whilst looking 'cute', they can dole out a mighty blow with their hind legs! The sturdy Dartmoor model has been around since medieval times but cross breeding has produced other strains. The Dartmoor Pony Society encourages attempts to maintain the purity of the breed. The foals, born in spring, are rounded up to be marked by their owners in the autumn. Sadly, these dear little creatures have now become a marketable product as horse meat.

Less visually pleasing than ponies are the cattle that graze on the Moor. Most of them are dully coloured and there is less demand for a photograph of a bovine beauty. The more popular breeds include Galloways, Aberdeen Angus, South Devon Cattle and Hereford Cross.

The first man to introduce 'Scotch' sheep onto Dartmoor was a Mr Lamb. Originally

introduced from the Scottish uplands, the sheep are hardy and need to be for a Dartmoor winter is always a severe test. Never try to be a good shepherd and pick up what may appear to be a lost lamb, sheep never wander very far and its mother will probably be close at hand. With the great number of visitors and Dartmoor Walkers around these days, it is very likely that any sheep finding it hard to sleep will try counting walkers climbing over gates!

Foxes are common on Dartmoor, both on the open Moors and in the woodlands but the casual visitor is most unlikely to see one of these cunning creatures. Incidentally, the Belstone Fox had nothing to do with the village of Belstone on Dartmoor

The buzzard, another predator, will often be seen hunting on the Moors and ravens and kestrels will often be spied in the vicinity of a tor, a favoured habitat for nesting. Herons favour a watery environment to indulge in their favourite pastime of fishing. Other birds, which may be spotted on the Moors, include skylarks, meadow pipits, windchats, stonechats, short eared owls, snipe and the wheatear. It is believed that the latter is more commonly found on Dartmoor than anywhere else in this country. The woodland birds include warblers, redstarts, tits, woodpeckers, dippers, wagtails and sandpiper amongst many others.

Obviously there are many other creatures not listed but, like all the topics in this publication, a book could be written about each different aspect (and probably has been).

WALKING ON THE MOORS

There are two distinct types of Dartmoor Walker, (1) who dons all the gear, has the right maps, knows how to use a compass and is fit to face any situation and (2) the novice who sees an attractive rockpile at the top of a hill and decides to go 'walkies'. (1) rarely gets into trouble and thoroughly enjoys the excursion, but (2) invariably gets caught out and wishes he hadn't started.

Dartmoor weather is so unpredictable and can change so suddenly that an all-veiling mist can totally mask the landscape in minutes. A person can be within yards of their vehicle and still miss it. Dartmoor can be a death trap and respect for it needs to be shown at all times. If you are an inexperienced walker you might try a guided walk. The Dartmoor National Park employs expert guides and any of their many information centres will furnish details of the walks.

For the experienced enthusiast the Moor offers some incredible sights. It has been described as The Last Great Wilderness of England and the starkness and remoteness of the high Northern Moors and the bog-infested raised plateau of the Southern Moors provide the perfect environment from which to escape the rigours and stresses of modern living. However the Armed Forces use a vast area of the Northern Moor for firing practice and other exercises. The local press carries warning notices every

Friday and these give the extent of the three ranges at Okehampton, Willsworthy and Merrivale. There is usually no firing in August and most weekends are clear. An 'ansafone' service under 'Army' gives the same information so always check first and never pick up metal objects, unless of course they are ...

DARTMOOR LETTERBOXES

The ordinary visitor to Dartmoor may well not wish to explore the more inaccessible parts of the Moor away from the road, but they may find the subject of Dartmoor Letterboxes just tempting enough to want to walk. Hidden in out-of-the-way places you may find receptacles of various shapes and sizes that usually contain a visitors' book for names, addresses and silly comments (the sillier the better it seems) and a rubber stamp with a design to reflect the name of the location. It is the latter that is the main attraction and dedicated followers will put up with the most atrocious conditions imaginable in their quest to find 'boxes'.

The 'hobby' was unwittingly born in 1854 when James Perrot, a famous Dartmoor guide from Chagford, set up a bottle at Cranmere Pool for visitors to leave their calling cards. After decades when the only other boxes were at Belstone Tor, Crow Tor, Ducks Pool and Fur Tor, the number of boxes has now reached enormous proportions. It is quite common for enthusiasts to have visited more than a thousand different locations with several chunky volumes full of different letterbox designs. Boxers too carry their own personal rubber stamps, which are highly collectible items, and they give themselves nicknames like 'Pensioned Plodder', 'The Tor Mentors', 'The Dartmoor Carter-Piller' and many more. It has a tremendous cult following.

Many of the rubber stamps cost a lot of money and there are some beautiful designs. Someone with a good collection will have stamps that depict events, rivers, bogs, tors, industry and so on. Letterboxing brings people together and enhances the enjoyment of Dartmoor for thousands of walkers. If you see people going through a ritual of searching rigorously around a tor or disused quarry you can be sure that they are 'boxers' and most of them are friendly folk.

Well, that's about all the room we have. Inevitably, in a book this size, we can only touch on any topic, but we hope that you have enjoyed this brief introduction to Dartmoor.